P9-BIF-971

NIGHT SKIES of CANADA

Tamara Hartson

The Night Sky

When we look into the night sky we can see the stars of outer space. Stars are always present in the sky, but we cannot see them during the day because of the light from the Sun.

The planet Earth is in space, just like the sun and the moon.

Even though the **night sky** looks like it is full of stars, it is really quite empty. The distance between stars in space is very far.

We can see many interesting things in the **night sky**, such as **planets**, **stars**, **comets**, **nebulas**, **meteors** and **galaxies**.

Astronomers use special computers and telescopes to learn about stars and other objects in space.

People used to think Earth was the center of the universe. Nicolaus Copernicus was one of the first astronomers to say that Earth revolves around the Sun.

A long time ago, Galileo Galilei used his telescope to see the movement of the planets. He also discovered the 4 largest moons of Jupiter.

Astronomers

Sky Watching

The night sky has more than just stars to see. We can see planets, meteors, the moon, star clusters and even other galaxies!

With a telescope, you can even see the rings of Saturn.

Use binoculars at twilight to view the craters of the moon. At night, you can also see the 4 largest moons of Jupiter!

Inner city sky	Suburban sky	Countryside sky

For the best sky watching, try to avoid cities. Countrysides and wilderness offer the best dark skies for star gazing!

Sunset

To watch the night sky, begin at sunset. This is the best time to view the moon. When the sky is completely dark, the moon is too bright to see the craters on its surface.

The first star visible after sunset is the planet Venus.

When the glowing sun drops below the horizon, the sun is said to have set. The time after the sun has set but before the sky is completely dark is called twilight.

Right after the sun sets there can be a rare flash of light called the Green Flash. This Green Flash is easiest to see over the ocean or open landscapes like grasslands.

The aurora borealis is also known as northern lights. Auroras are caused by particles from the sun mixing with Earth's magnetic field, which is like an invisible shield surrounding our planet. Winter is the best time to see an aurora.

Aurora Borealis

Auroras are mostly green, but sometimes they are red, pink, white, violet or blue!

Auroras are common around the north and south poles. An aurora at the south pole is called aurora australis.

Auroras also make sounds. On a quiet night you may hear snapping, clapping, or crackling sounds.

Tycho Crater

Earth's moon, called Luna, is full of craters from asteroid impacts. One of the easiest craters to recognize is Tycho crater. The rays around the crater were caused by bits of rock being thrown out in a circle when the asteroid hit.

The Moon

The moon glows because the sun shines on it. As the moon revolves around Earth, we see different parts of the sunlit moon. These are known as the phases of the moon. The moon changes from a thin crescent to a full moon and back again every month.

Waxing Crescent (Getting bigger)

First Quarter Half Moon

Waxing Gibbous Moon

New Moon (Moon is not visible)

Full Moon

Here are all the phases of the moon.

Waning Crescent

Third Quarter Half Moon

Waning Gibbous Moon (Getting smaller)

The Sun is the closest star to Earth. Light from the sun takes 8 minutes and 20 seconds to reach Earth. The next closest star to Earth is called Proxima Centauri. Light from this star takes more than 4 years to reach Earth!

Stars

A star is a hot sphere of glowing gas. Stars produce heat, light and energy. The planets in our Solar System are sometimes called stars because we see them as dots of light in the night sky.

Some of the stars in the night sky are actually other galaxies. They are so far away they appear to us as a single point of light.

Galaxies & Star Clusters

Andromeda

We can easily see the spiral shape of the Andromeda galaxy with a telescope.

Messier 92

The spherical Messier 92 star cluster is located within our Milky Way galaxy.

The Milky Way

Our Solar System is in a galaxy called the Milky Way. On a clear night far away from any city lights, you can see a thick band of stars. This is the Milky Way.

Planets

Our Solar System has 8 planets, 5 dwarf planets and many small minor planets that may soon be counted as dwarf planets. Some planets are visible as stars at night. With binoculars or a telecsope, it is possible to see some details of the planets.

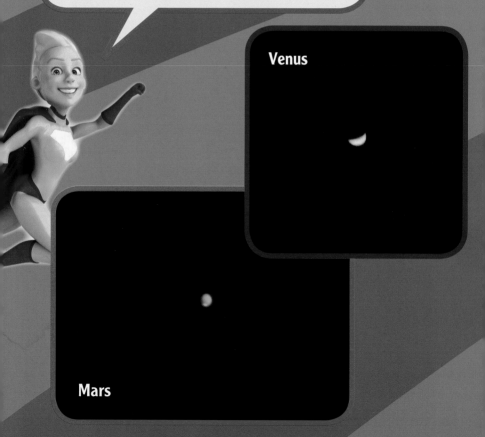

Venus

Mars

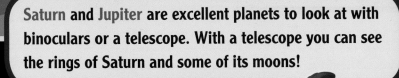

Saturn and Jupiter are excellent planets to look at with binoculars or a telescope. With a telescope you can see the rings of Saturn and some of its moons!

Saturn

Jupiter has 69 moons! The 4 largest are called the Galilean Moons. You can easily see them with binoculars or with a telescope.

Jupiter

Nebulas

Nebulas are large clouds of dust and gases in space. Sometimes so much gas and dust collects that stars can form inside the clouds.

Orion Nebula

Lagoon Nebula

With binoculars or a telescope, you can see the Orion Nebula on the sword of Orion's belt and the Lagoon Nebula near the constellation Sagittarius.

Comets are like big, dirty snowballs. They are mostly made of ice, dust and rock. The tail of the comet is made of dust and gas.

The main part of the comet can be as small as a football field or as big as a city!

When a comet is close to Earth, we can see it in the night sky. Halley's Comet passes by Earth every 75 years. Comet McNaught, shown here, passed Earth in 2007.

Comets

Meteors & Meteor Showers

A meteor shower happens when Earth moves through a region of space with lots of asteroids and meteoroids. When they pass through the Earth's atmosphere, the chunks burn up. The burning trail visible from Earth is called a meteor. When a meteor hits the Earth it is called a meteorite.

Meteor showers happen
several times each year.
The best meteor showers are:
- the Perseids in August,
- the Orionids in October,
- the Leonids in November,
- the Geminids in December.

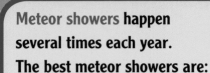

Some people
call meteors
shooting stars.

Constellations

A **constellation** is a fairly close group of stars that form a pattern. We use imaginary lines or figures to represent these patterns. The figures are usually animals, mythological creatures or gods, or devices. There are 88 official constellations.

Zodiac

The **zodiac** refers to 12 constellations that appear on the same level as the Earth's orbit around the sun (the **elliptic**). Most of these are animal constellations. The word "zodiac" comes from Greek and means "circle of little animals."

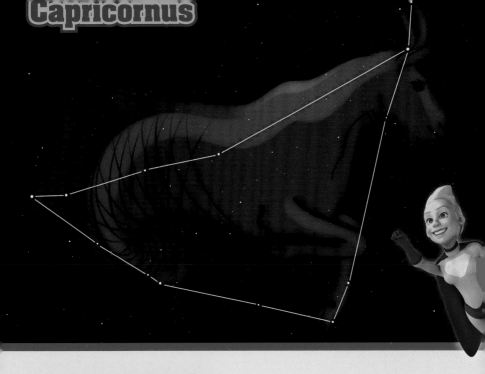

Best season for viewing:
FALL

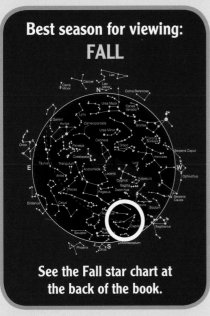

See the Fall star chart at the back of the book.

Capricornus (the Sea Goat)

Capricornus is the smallest constellation in the zodiac. The stars of Capricornus are faint, so it is best to look for this constellation away from city lights. People have identified this triangular pattern for nearly 4 thousand years. Capricornus is a goat and represents the Greek god Pan. Legend says that Pan grew a fish tail to swim fast in order to flee the sea monster Typhon.

Aquarius

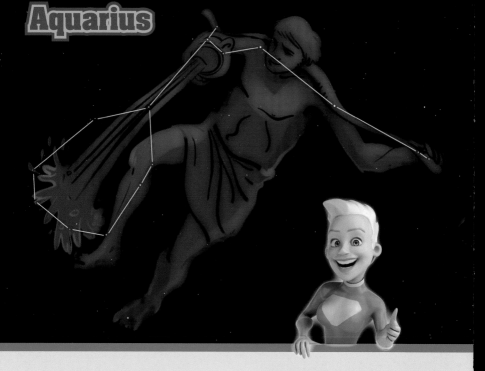

Aquarius (the Water Bearer)
Aquarius is a faint constellation next to Capricornus. The pattern represents Ganymede, a young hero in Greek mythology. He is the cup bearer to the gods and pours water out of a jug. Ganymede is also the name of the largest moon of Jupiter, one that can be seen with binoculars. Powerful telescopes have found a bean-shaped galaxy in Aquarius that glows green!

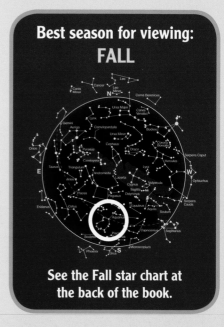

Best season for viewing:
FALL

See the Fall star chart at the back of the book.

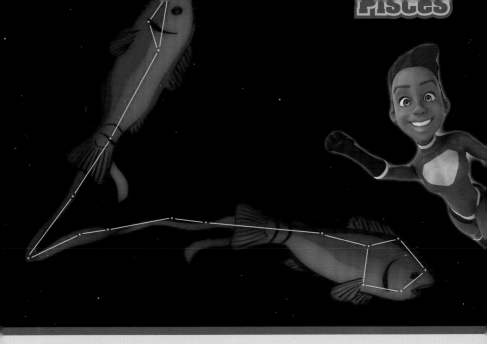

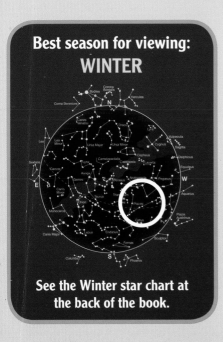

Best season for viewing:
WINTER

See the Winter star chart at the back of the book.

Pisces (the Fishes)

This constellation has been recognized for thousands of years. The two fish represent Aphrodite, the Greek goddess of love, and her son, Eros. To escape a many-headed sea monster, they changed into fish and dove into the sea. They tied a rope between their tails to stay together.

Aries (the Ram)

This simple pattern of stars represents a male sheep, called a ram. In Greek mythology, Aries is the ram that has golden fleece (wool). Golden fleece is a symbol of kings and authority. The ram was sacrificed to Poseidon, the God of the Sea and so took a place in the sky. The golden fleece was then hung on a tree and protected by a dragon that never sleeps.

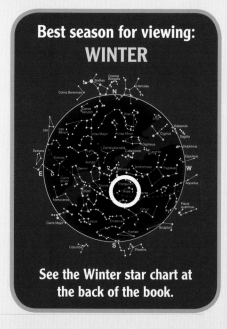

Best season for viewing:
WINTER

See the Winter star chart at the back of the book.

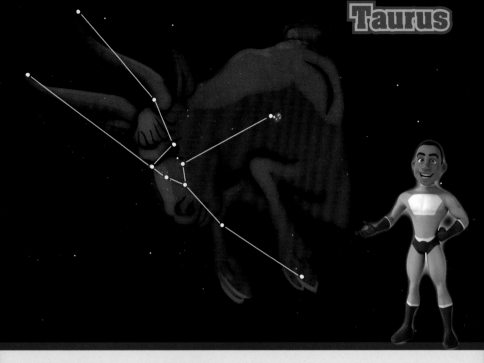

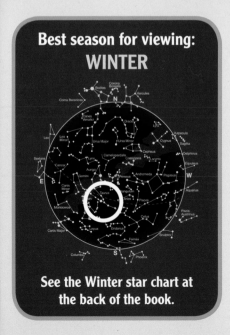

Best season for viewing:
WINTER

See the Winter star chart at
the back of the book.

Taurus (the Bull)

Taurus is a constellation with the figure of a bull. It is one of the animals in the sky that is hunted by Orion, the great hunter. Within Taurus is the star cluster called Pleiades. The Pleiades is the best example of a star cluster that is visible to the naked eye. During October, the Taurid Meteor Shower comes from the general direction of this constellation.

Gemini

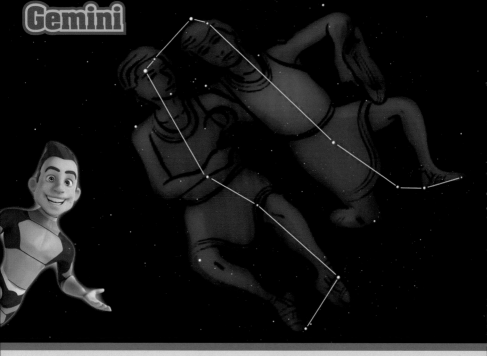

Gemini (the Twins)

Gemini represents twin brothers, Castor and Pollux, figures from Greek mythology. When Castor was killed, Pollux asked his father, Zeus, to share immortality with his departed twin. They were transformed into the Gemini constellation to stay in the sky forever. During December, the Geminid Meteor Shower comes from the general direction of this constellation.

Best season for viewing:
SPRING

See the Spring star chart at the back of the book.

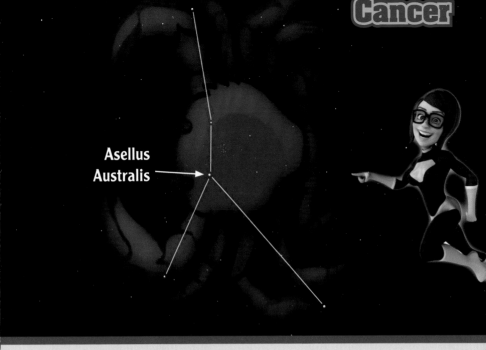

Asellus
Australis

Best season for viewing:
SPRING

**See the Spring star chart at
the back of the book.**

Cancer (the Crab)

**This constellation shows a crab. In
Greek mythology, when Hercules
was fighting a many-headed
monster called Hydra, a giant crab
came to distract Hercules and help
Hydra. Hercules crushed the crab
with his foot, and the crab was
placed in the sky. The arrow
points to the star Asellus Australis.
The original name for this star
is the longest star name of all:
Arkushanangarushashutu.**

Leo

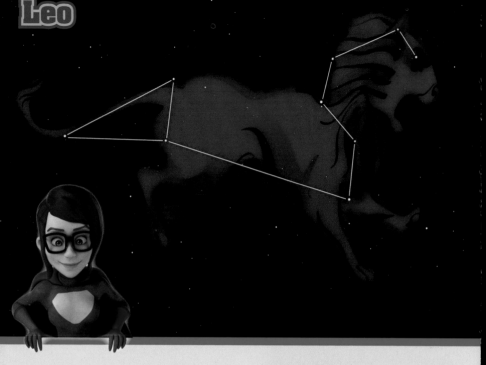

Leo (the Lion)

Leo is a constellation that shows the fierce lion of Greek mythology. This lion had golden fur that could not be pierced by any weapon and had claws sharper than any sword. Hercules came to kill the lion, but realized he had to strangle it with his bare hands. The lion was then placed among the stars. During November, the Leonid Meteor Shower comes from the general direction of this constellation.

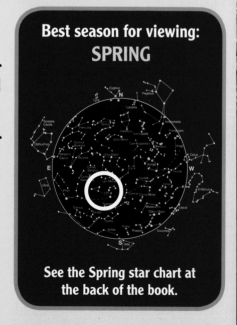

Best season for viewing:
SPRING

See the Spring star chart at the back of the book.

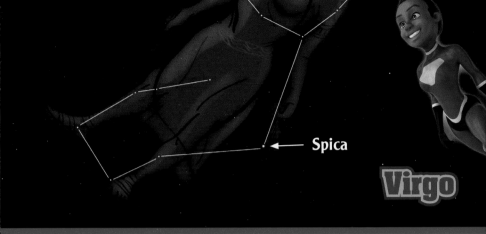

Spica

Virgo

Best season for viewing:
SUMMER

See the Summer star chart at
the back of the book.

Virgo (the Maiden)
Virgo is the largest constellation of the zodiac and the second largest of all 88 constellations. This pattern represents a young woman. In Greek mythology, she is the goddess of wheat and agriculture. The star that marks the wheat in her hand is Spica, one of the brightest stars in the night sky.

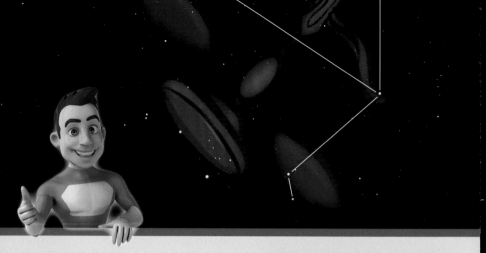

Libra (the Balance)

Libra is a faint constellation that represents an old-fashioned scale. Many cultures use the scale to stand for justice and truth. Libra is the only constellation of the zodiac that represents a device instead of a person or animal. Three of the stars in the Libra constellation are known to have planets.

Best season for viewing:
SUMMER

See the Summer star chart at the back of the book.

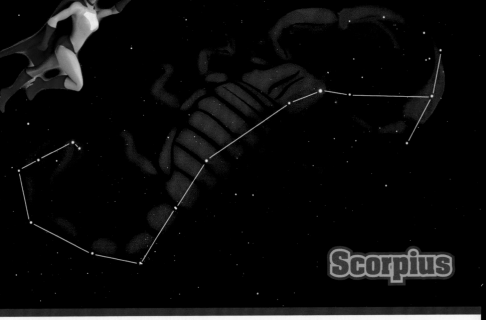

Scorpius

Scorpius (the Scorpion)

This pattern of stars is known as the Scorpion. In Greek mythology, Orion claimed he was such a good hunter he could kill every animal on Earth. Artemis, the goddess of wild animals and wilderness, wanted to protect all creatures and sent a scorpion to kill Orion. After the battle, both were raised into the heavens.

Best season for viewing:
SUMMER

See the Summer star chart at the back of the book.

Sagittarius

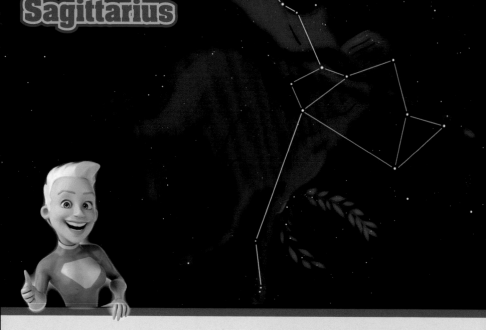

Sagittarius (the Archer)

In Greek mythology, this constellation represents the centaur, a creature that is half human and half horse. Sagittarius is the archer, and his bow and arrow are ready to shoot. Legend says that he is aiming at Scorpius to avenge the death of Orion. The part of Sagittarius shown with orange lines is known as the "Teapot."

Best season for viewing:
SUMMER

See the Summer star chart at the back of the book.

Great Bear

Great Bear (Ursa Major)
The Big Dipper portion of this constellation, shown in orange, is one of the most well-known of all star patterns and is visible for most of the year. The shape of the dipper resembles a ladle. The complete figure shows a female bear. Two of the stars in the dipper part (connected with a green line) point to Polaris, the North Star. Polaris is part of a constellation called the Little Bear.

Best season for viewing:
SPRING

See the Spring star chart at the back of the book.

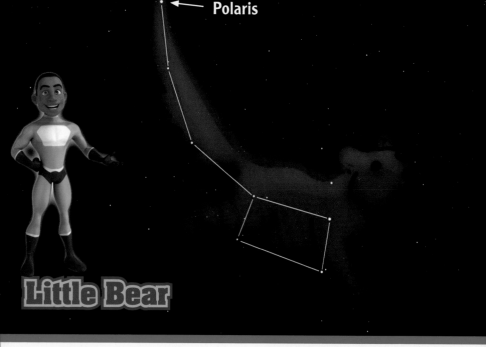

Polaris

Little Bear

Little Bear (Ursa Minor)

The Little Bear, or Little Dipper, contains Polaris, the North Star. Polaris is the first star of the tail. Stars in the sky move in a circle, but Polaris is the north pole of the sky, so it stays still. Explorers have always used Polaris to find their way. First Nations people say the three stars of the tail represent the Wolf, Fox and Coyote, and the four stars of the "dipper" are four sets of pups.

Best season for viewing:
SUMMER

See the Summer star chart at the back of the book.

Best season for viewing:
WINTER

See the Winter star chart at the back of the book.

The Queen (Cassiopeia)
This constellation is easy to find because it is the zig-zag or W-shaped group of stars. The figure represents Queen Cassiopeia from Greek mythology. She was placed in the sky by Poseidon as punishment for boasting of her great beauty. She sits on her throne beside Cepheus, the King, and Andromeda, her daughter.

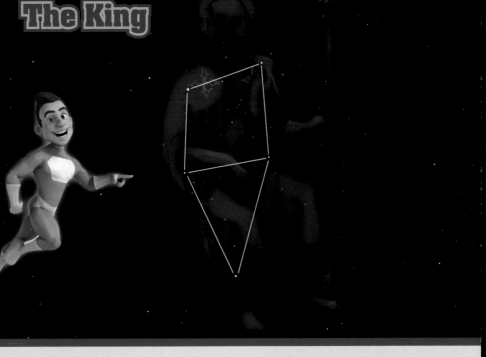

The King

The King (Cepheus)

In Greek mythology **King Cepheus** is the husband of **Cassiopeia** and the father of **Andromeda**. Legend says that Cassiopeia bragged of her own and Andromeda's beauty, which angered **Poseidon**. Poseidon demanded their sacrifice in order for Cepheus to save his kingdom. Later, Cepheus was lifted into the heavens by Zeus. This constellation is near **Polaris**, the North Star, and is visible all year.

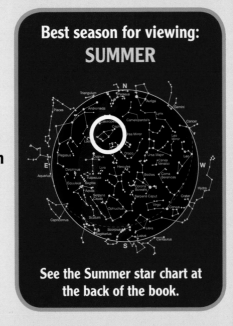

Best season for viewing:
SUMMER

See the Summer star chart at the back of the book.

The Chained Princess (Andromeda)

Best season for viewing:
FALL

See the Fall star chart at the back of the book.

This large constellation is easy to find in the autumn sky. Andromeda is the daughter of Queen Cassiopeia and King Cepheus. Greek legend says that she was chained to a rock to be sacrificed to a sea monster because her mother bragged of her beauty. Perseus, the Hero, rescued her, and they later married.

Hero (Perseus)

Perseus is the hero in Greek mythology. He killed Medusa, the monster who had snakes for hair. Anyone who looked at Medusa turned to stone. Perseus also rescued Andromeda, the princess that was chained to rocks as a sacrifice to a sea monster. Perseus can be seen overhead in the winter. In August, the Perseid Meteor Shower comes from the general direction of this constellation.

Best season for viewing:
WINTER

See the Winter star chart at the back of the book.

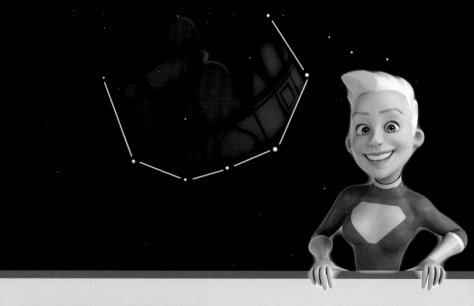

Best season for viewing:
SUMMER

See the Summer star chart at the back of the book.

The Crown (Corona Borealis) This simple constellation resembles a crown. In Greek mythology, it is the crown that a god gave to princess Ariadne. They married, and the god put the crown in the sky to celebrate their wedding. Some First Nations people see these 7 stars as 7 birds that chased and killed the Great Bear (Ursa Major). Others see the Crown as a dome resembling a sweat lodge.

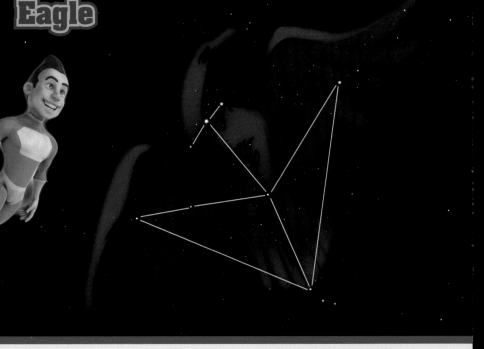

Eagle

Eagle (Aquila)

The Eagle is a triangular pattern of stars in the summer and autumn sky. Greek legends say that this is the eagle that belonged to Zeus and that held his thunderbolts. At the command of Zeus, the eagle also carried Ganymede (Aquarius) to Mount Olympus, the home of the gods.

Best season for viewing:
FALL

See the Fall star chart at the back of the book.

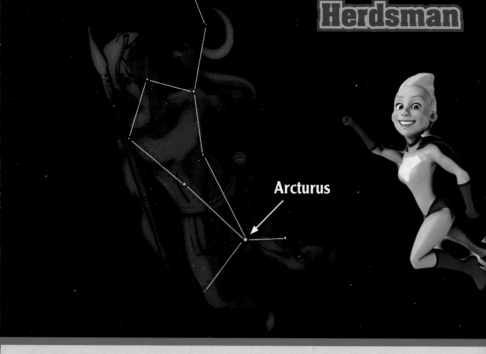

Arcturus

Best season for viewing:
SUMMER

See the Summer star chart at
the back of the book.

Herdsman (Boötes)

Many stories exist about this constellation. The most common story is that Boötes is the herder that keeps all the animals of the sky together. The arrow points to one of the brightest stars in the sky within this constellation. This bright, orange star is Arcturus. Some First Nations people called this constellation the Fish Trap.

Swan

Swan (Cygnus)

This cross-shaped constellation is easy to find in the fall. Greek legend says that Zeus disguised himself as a swan to win the heart of princess Leda. Leda is the mother of Castor and Pollux, the twins of the Gemini constellation. Some First Nations people call this pattern Niska, the wild goose. The Milky Way is called the "Summer Birds Path," and Niska follows this path while migrating.

Best season for viewing:
FALL

See the Fall star chart at the back of the book.

Dragon

Best season for viewing:
SUMMER

See the Summer star chart at the back of the book.

Dragon (Draco)

The Dragon constellation can be seen all year, but is easiest to see in summer because it is directly overhead. Greek legend says that this is the dragon Ladon, who guarded golden apples in a beautiful garden. Hercules had to steal the golden apples, and to do so he had to slay the dragon. The constellation Hercules is right beside the dragon.

Hercules

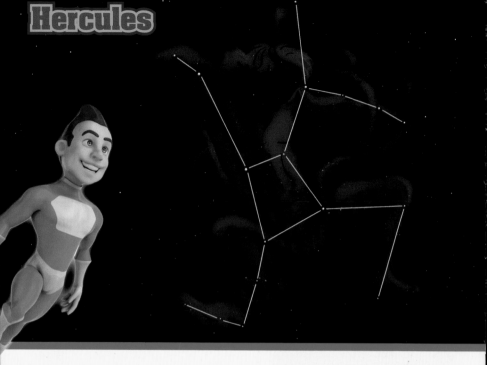

Hercules

One of the greatest heroes in mythology, Hercules is known as the monster killer. He slayed many creatures, including Draco (the dragon), Leo (the lion), Hydra (a many-headed monster) and Cancer (the crab). He was accidentally poisoned by his wife, and when he died, the god Zeus placed him in the sky.

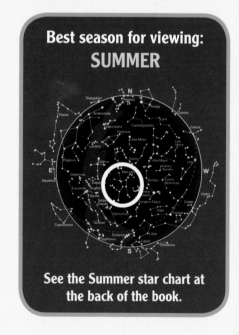

Best season for viewing:
SUMMER

See the Summer star chart at the back of the book.

Best season for viewing:
WINTER

See the Winter star chart at the back of the book.

Giraffe (Camelopardalis)
This is a fairly newly described constellation, so it does not follow any story from mythology. "Camelopardalis" is the Latin name for a giraffe. The name comes from "camel" and "pardalis," which refers to a giraffe having spots like a leopard. Voyager I, a space probe NASA sent out in 1977, is heading towards the stars in the Giraffe.

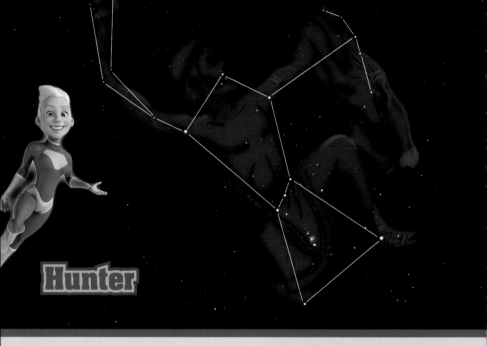

Hunter

Hunter (Orion)

The pattern of stars that makes Orion is the oldest and most widely recognized constellation. Cave art from more than 30,000 years ago show these same stars. Orion was the great hunter in Greek Mythology and battled with Scorpius (the scorpion.) During late October, the Orionid Meteor Shower comes from the general direction of the Orion constellation.

Best season for viewing:
WINTER

See the Winter star chart at the back of the book.

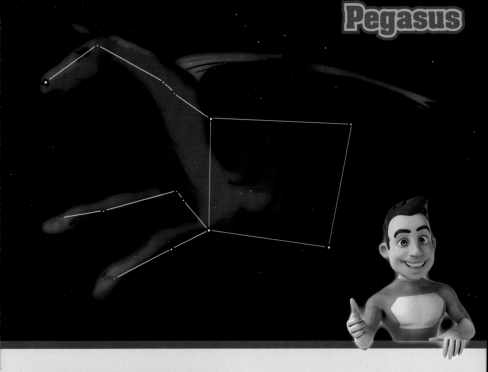

Pegasus

Best season for viewing:
FALL

See the Fall star chart at
the back of the book.

Pegasus

This constellation is easily recognizable because of the Square of Pegasus, shown in orange. In Greek mythology, Pegasus is the inspiration for poetry. Pegasus is the winged horse that brought thunder and lightning from Mount Olympus to the god Zeus. One of the stars in Pegasus was the first star discovered to be like our Sun with a planet circling it.

Sunrise

The last of the night sky watching ends with sunrise. Like sunset, it is a good time to view the moon with binoculars. Sometimes there is even a Green Flash before the sun rises.

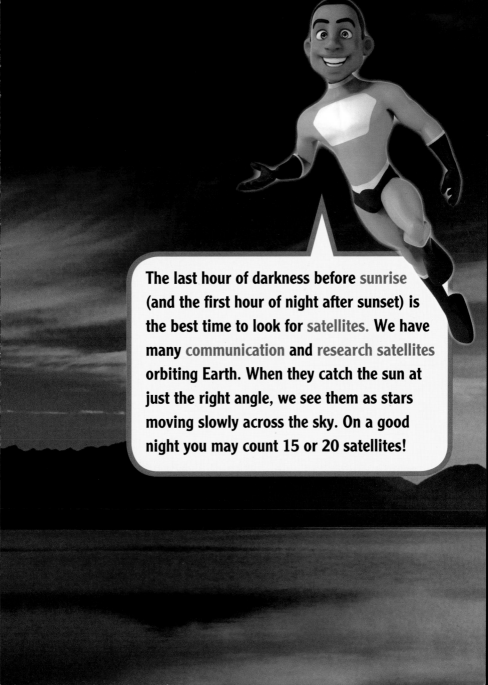

The last hour of darkness before sunrise (and the first hour of night after sunset) is the best time to look for satellites. We have many communication and research satellites orbiting Earth. When they catch the sun at just the right angle, we see them as stars moving slowly across the sky. On a good night you may count 15 or 20 satellites!

Spring

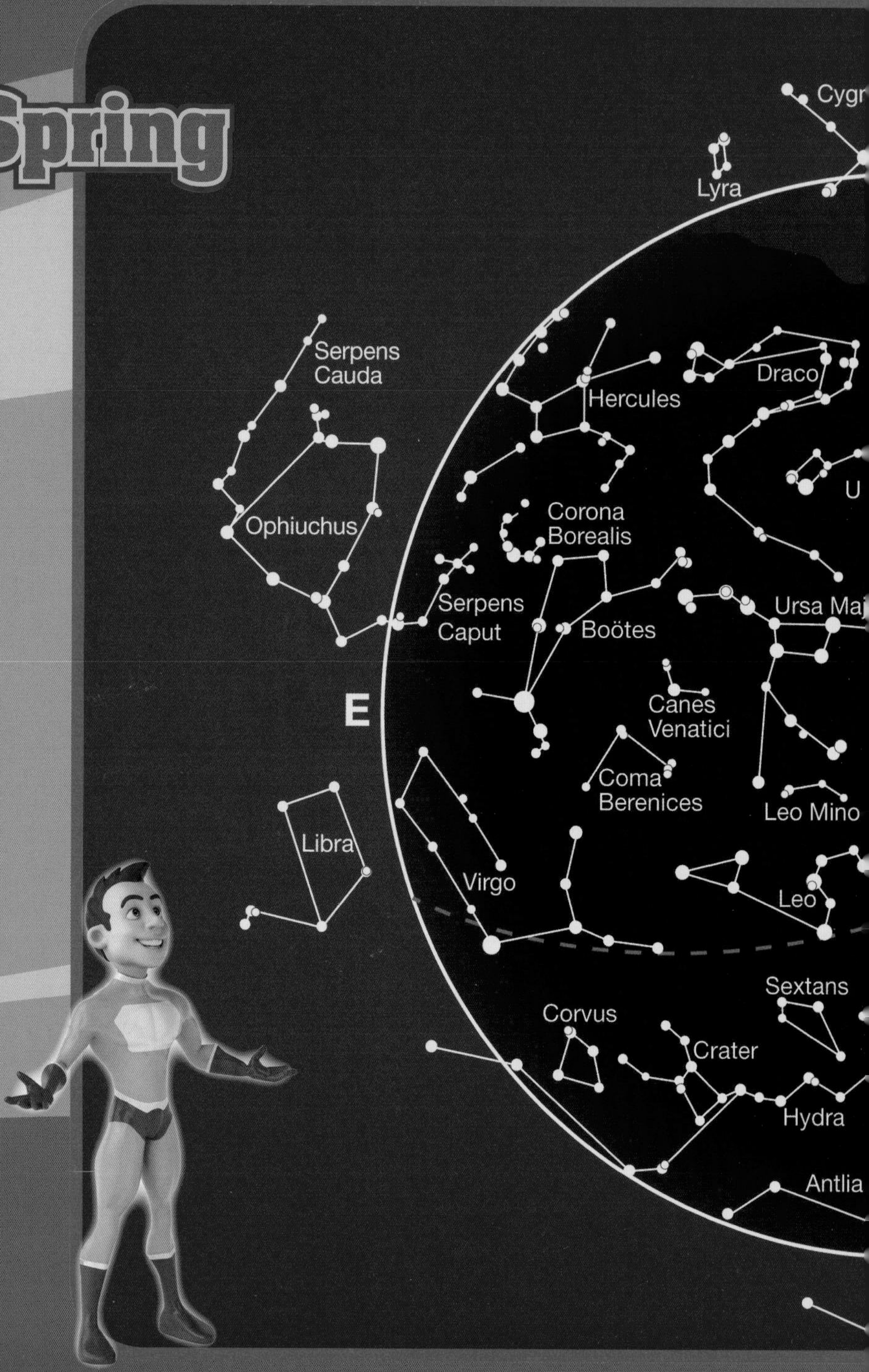

Cygr

Lyra

Serpens
Cauda

Hercules

Draco

U

Ophiuchus

Corona
Borealis

Serpens
Caput

Boötes

Ursa Maj

E

Canes
Venatici

Coma
Berenices

Leo Mino

Libra

Virgo

Leo

Corvus

Crater

Sextans

Hydra

Antlia

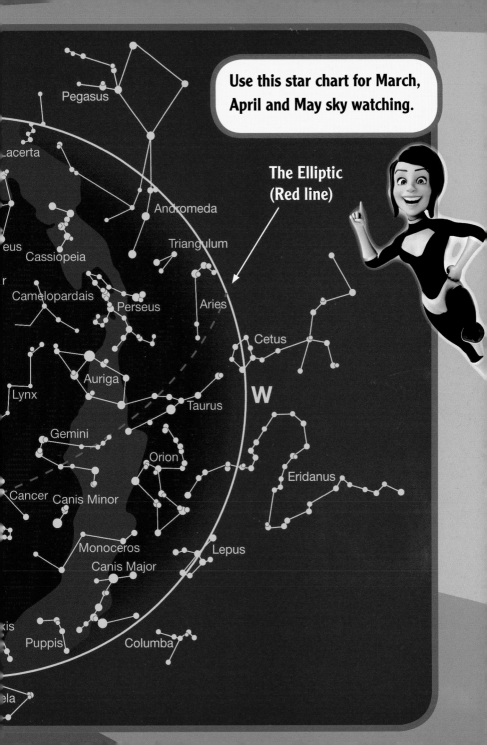

Use this star chart for March, April and May sky watching.

The Elliptic
(Red line)

Pegasus

Lacerta

Andromeda

eus

Cassiopeia

Triangulum

Camelopardais

Perseus

Aries

Cetus

Auriga

Lynx

Taurus

W

Gemini

Orion

Eridanus

Cancer

Canis Minor

Monoceros

Lepus

Canis Major

xis

Puppis

Columba

ela

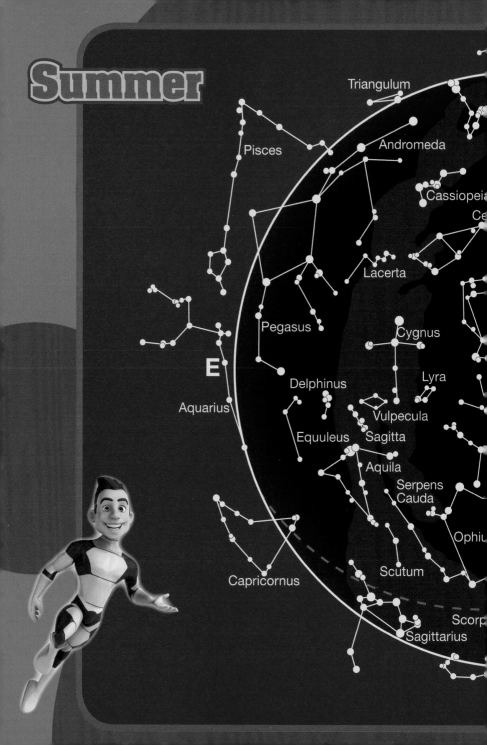

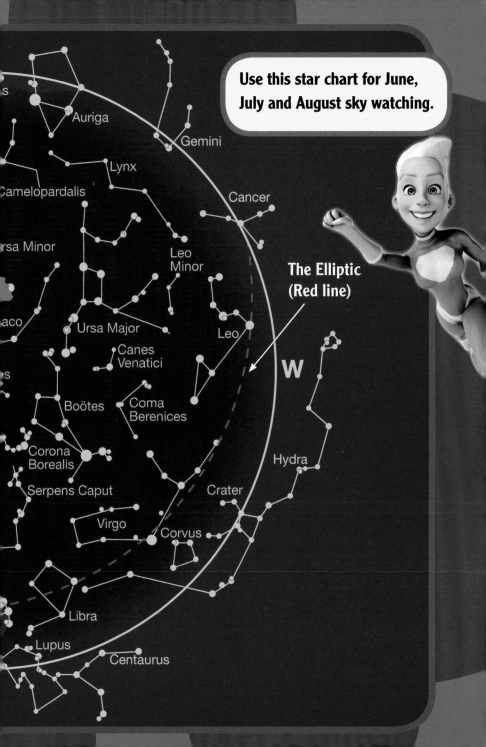

Use this star chart for June, July and August sky watching.

The Elliptic (Red line)

Auriga
Gemini
Lynx
Camelopardalis
Cancer
rsa Minor
Leo Minor
aco
Ursa Major
Leo
Canes Venatici
W
Boötes
Coma Berenices
Corona Borealis
Hydra
Serpens Caput
Crater
Virgo
Corvus
Libra
Lupus
Centaurus

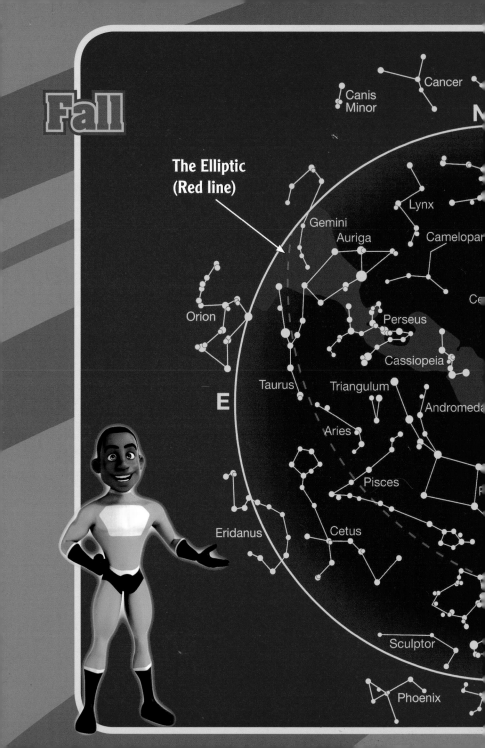

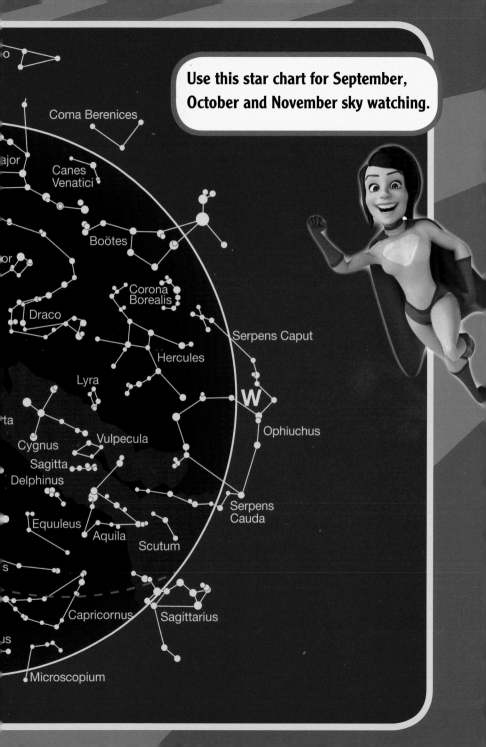

Use this star chart for September, October and November sky watching.

Coma Berenices

ajor

Canes
Venatici

Boötes

or

Corona
Borealis

Draco

Serpens Caput

Hercules

Lyra

W

ta

Cygnus

Vulpecula

Ophiuchus

Sagitta

Delphinus

Equuleus

Serpens
Cauda

Aquila

Scutum

s

Capricornus

Sagittarius

us

Microscopium

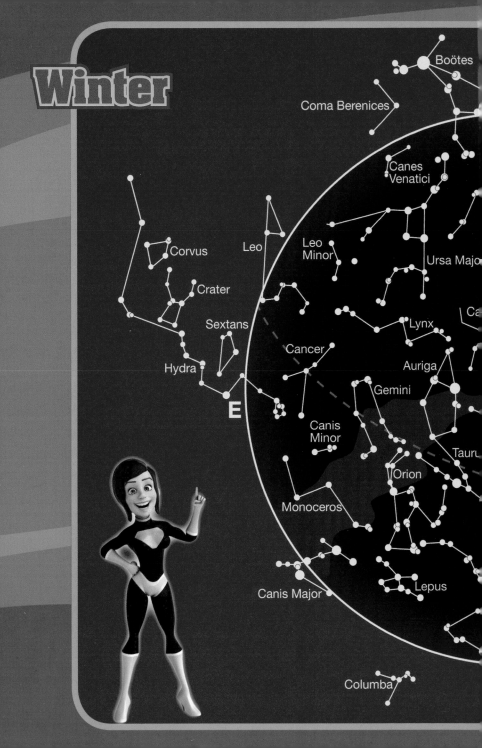

Winter

Boötes

Coma Berenices

Canes
Venatici

Corvus

Leo

Leo
Minor

Ursa Majo

Crater

Ca

Sextans

Lynx

Hydra

Cancer

Auriga

E

Gemini

Canis
Minor

Taur

Orion

Monoceros

Lepus

Canis Major

Columba

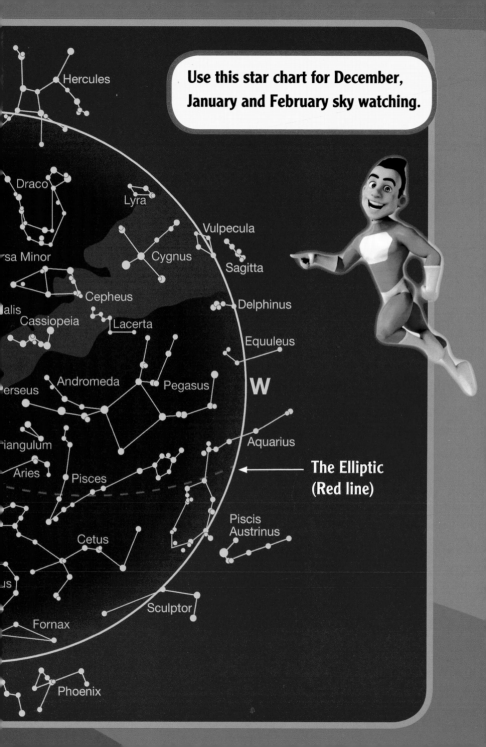

Use this star chart for December, January and February sky watching.

Hercules

Draco

Lyra

Vulpecula

sa Minor

Cygnus

Sagitta

Cepheus

Delphinus

alis

Cassiopeia

Lacerta

Equuleus

erseus

Andromeda

Pegasus

W

iangulum

Aquarius

Aries

Pisces

The Elliptic
(Red line)

Piscis
Austrinus

Cetus

us

Sculptor

Fornax

Phoenix

The Publisher: Super Explorers is an imprint of Blue Bike Books

Library and Archives Canada Cataloguing in Publication

Hartson, Tamara, 1974–, author
 Night skies of Canada / Tamara Hartson.

Issued in print and electronic formats.
ISBN 978-1-926700-86-1 (softcover).—ISBN 978-1-926700-87-8 (EPUB)

1. Astronomy—Juvenile literature. 2. Outer space—Juvenile literature. I. Title.

| QB500.22.H363 2018 | j520 | C2017-907086-X |
| | | C2017-907087-8 |

Front cover credit: den-belitsky, Thinkstock.

Back cover credits: trouvail, Thinkstock; adogslifephoto, Thinkstock; Johan Meuris, Stellarium.

Photo Credits: All photos are courtesy of NASA except for the following: From Wikimedia: Alvesgaspar 9a; Brocken Inaglory 9b; Dr. Baris Kececi 21b; Flameoffurius 15b; Hewholooks 16b; Manas shetty 21a; Navicore 25; NPS/Brad Sutton 16a; Ron Wayman 20b; Stellarium 7b; StudentAstronomyGroupUoC 22b; Takashi Hososhima 17a. From Thinkstock: adogslifephoto 18-19; ArildHeitmann 11b; Becart 13bDAJ 7a; knickohr 23b; Mumemories/Allexxandar 6-7; peresanz 22a; Photos.com 4b; Purestock 54-55; Romko_chuk 10-11; Stolk 4a; Terrance Emerson 8-9; valeriopardi 23a; vovik_mar 4b; wisanuboonrawd 24.

Illustrations: All constellation illustrations are courtesy of Johan Meuris, Stellarium. Star charts by Alesha Braitenbach-Cartledge.

Superhero Illustrations: julos/Thinkstock.

Produced with the assistance of the Government of Alberta. *Alberta* ◼
 Government

We acknowledge the financial support of the Government of Canada.
Nous reconnaissons l'appui financier du gouvernement du Canada.

Funded by the Government of Canada | **Canadä**
Financé par le gouvernement du Canada |

PC: 38